I0814443

THE MAGNIFICENT BOOK OF DOGS

THE MAGNIFICENT BOOK OF DOGS

ILLUSTRATED BY
Simon Treadwell

WRITTEN BY
Dr. Kim Dennis-Bryan

weldonowen

Written by Dr. Kim Dennis-Bryan
Illustrated by Simon Treadwell

weldon**owen**

Published by Weldon Owen Children's Books
An imprint of Weldon Owen International, L.P.
A subsidiary of Insight Editions
PO Box 3088
San Rafael, CA 94912
www.insighteditions.com

Weldon Owen Children's Books
Senior Designer: Emma Randall
Senior Editor: Pauline Savage
Editor: Eliza Kirby
Managing Editor: Mary Beth Garhart

Insight Editions
CEO: Raoul Goff
Senior Production Manager: Greg Steffen

ISBN: 979-8-88674-035-6

Manufactured in China by Insight Editions
First printing, June 2025. RRD0625
10 9 8 7 6 5 4 3 2 1

Insight Editions, in association with Roots of Peace, will plant two trees for each tree used in the manufacturing of this book.

The American Kennel Club is the largest purebred dog registry in the US. It is also the most influential dog club. The majority of measurements given in this book are in accordance with its standards. The American Kennel Club recognizes 202 breeds and divides them into seven groups—Hound, Working, Herding, Terrier, Sporting, Non-Sporting, and Toy.

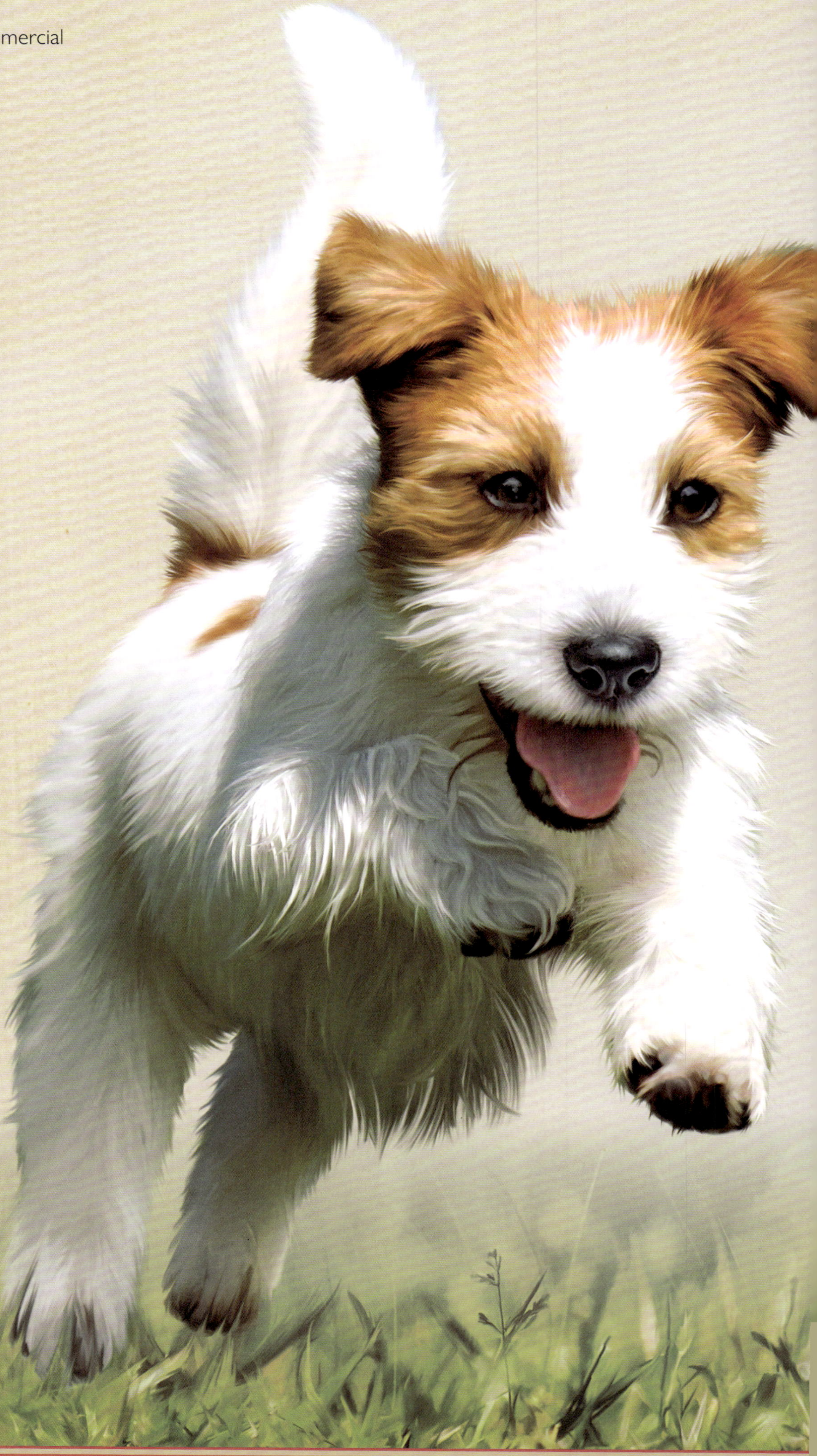

Introduction

Known as our "best friend," the dog is the oldest and most numerous of all household pets. Dogs started to live with people more than 14,000 years ago, when hunter-gatherers adopted the friendliest puppies of a now-extinct race of wolves that scavenged food from around their camps. Specific dog breeds appeared much later, with most being less than 250 years old. Nowadays, these breeds are grouped according to the tasks dogs were originally trained to do, such as herding livestock, hunting other animals, or just being companions.

Dogs vary more in shape and size than any other of our pets, and *The Magnificent Book of Dogs* introduces you to some of the most incredible ones. Meet the enormous Great Dane and Irish Wolfhound, which are the tallest dogs, as well as one of the shortest, the Dachshund. Marvel at the sleek Greyhound, the fastest dog, and the elegant Dalmatian, which has a unique spotted coat. Discover the fluffy Old English Sheepdog and the hairless Chinese Crested dog, one of the most unusual breeds because it has virtually no fur at all.

Learn about the amazing jobs that dogs have done, from finding injured soldiers on the battlefield to bringing back fishing nets in Canada. Discover the roles that some perform today, such as rescuing people from the water or being trusted guides for the blind.

Get ready to enter the magnificent realm of dogs as you explore some of the most fascinating breeds from around the world.

Fact file

Originates: England

Group: Terrier

Height: 10–12 in (25–30 cm)

Weight: 9–15 lb (4–7 kg)

Color: Mainly white with black and/or tan markings

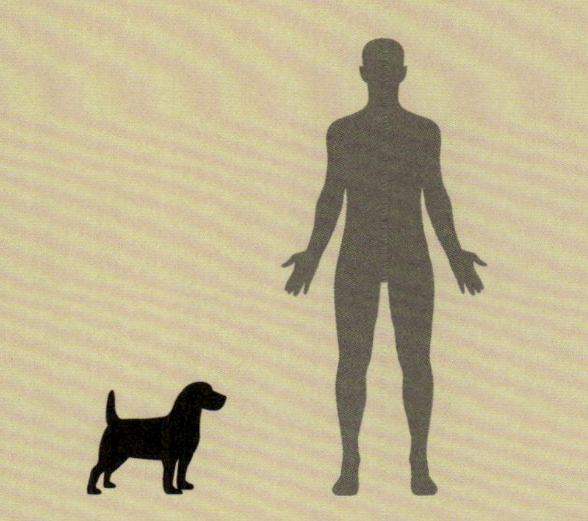

Contents

Golden Retriever

- Originally bred as gundogs, Golden Retrievers were used to bring waterfowl, such as ducks and geese, back to hunters. They were chosen for this work because they have "soft mouths," meaning they could carry the birds gently without leaving bite marks or damaging them.

- Sensible, intelligent, good-natured, and kind are just a few of the qualities that make Golden Retrievers popular family pets. They love people and are good with children.

- Golden Retrievers are tolerant and easy to train. This makes them well-suited to being guide dogs for the blind or therapy dogs.

- Golden Retrievers have medium-length coats with feathering, or longer hair, on their legs and tail. They shed hair all year but lose larger amounts in spring when their thick winter undercoat thins out.

A Golden Retriever's bark can be quite loud. An Australian dog named Charlie registered 113.1 decibels in a barking competition—the same volume as a loud rock concert.

Fact file

Originates: Scotland

Group: Sporting

Height:
Females 21½–22½ in (54.5–57 cm)
Males 23–24 in (58–61 cm)

Weight:
Females 55–65 lb (25–30 kg)
Males 65–75 lb (30–35 kg)

Color: Rich golden shades

French Bulldog

- French Bulldogs are easy to identify because of their large, batlike ears and very short tails. They are one of the most popular breeds of dog.

- This compact and solid dog has a rounded head and relatively short nose. It also has large eyes and a lower jaw that is slightly undershot, meaning it is longer than the upper jaw.

- The faces of some fawn French Bulldogs have a black mask that covers the muzzle and sometimes the eyes as well.

- French Bulldogs make affectionate, loyal, and entertaining pets that are equally at home in a town or in the country. They can sometimes be stubborn but, with patience, can be trained to obey instructions.

- The breed probably originated from the small British Bulldogs that were taken to northern France in the 1850s by lacemakers from Nottingham. During the Industrial Revolution, many lacemakers emigrated to Europe in search of work, taking their dogs with them.

Fact file

Originates: France
Group: Non-Sporting
Height: 11–13 in (28–33 cm)
Weight: Up to 28 lb (12.5 kg)
Color: White, cream, fawn; markings can be pied or brindle

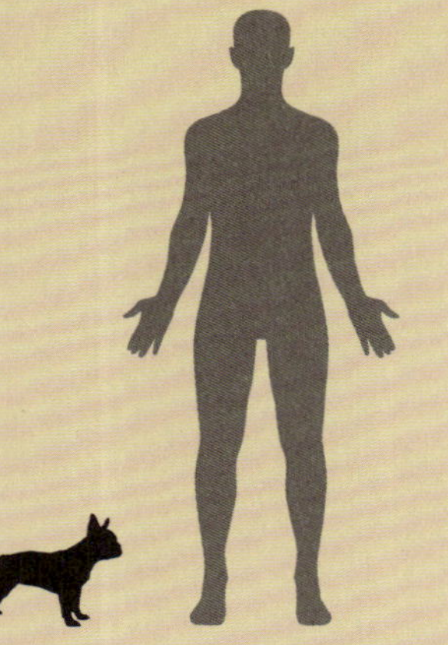

- The French Bulldog became very popular in Paris in the late 1800s. Owning one was considered the height of fashion.

- The famous French artists Edgar Degas and Henri de Toulouse-Lautrec both painted French Bulldogs. In 1897, Toulouse-Lautrec made a portrait of Bouboule, a dog belonging to a woman named Madame Palmyre. She was one of the first members of the French Bulldog Owners Club.

Afghan Hound

- The Afghan Hound is a large, energetic dog that is known for its long, luxurious coat. It loves to run around and play games.
- The Afghan Hound is a sighthound that uses its eyes rather than its nose when hunting. Many sighthounds come from the dry areas of Asia and Africa, where there are very few trees and plants to block their view.
- Afghan Hounds are fast runners, reaching speeds of 40 mph (65 km/h) over short distances. Like Greyhounds, they are used for racing.
- In their homeland, Afghan Hounds were once used to hunt mammals ranging in size from hares to antelopes and deer. As soon as they spotted an animal, they used their speed to run it down.

Fact file

Originates: Afghanistan

Group: Hound

Height:
Females 24–26 in (61–66 cm)
Males 26–28 in (66–71 cm)

Weight:
Females about 50 lb (23 kg)
Males about 60 lb (27 kg)

Color: All colors

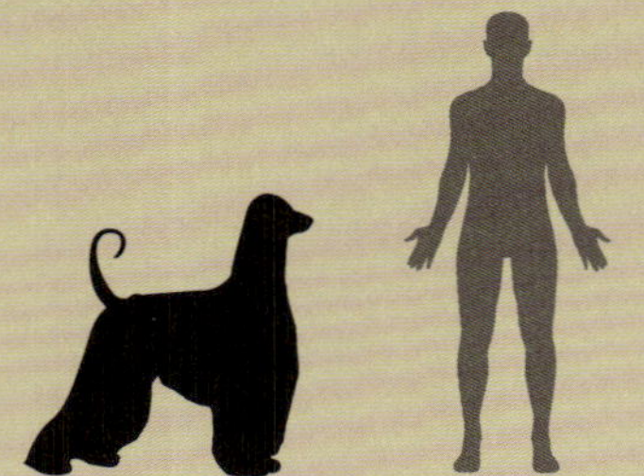

- There is a legend in Afghanistan that a pair of Afghan Hounds were chosen for Noah's Ark. They were among the last animals to board and so were standing near the ark's door. During the flood that followed, the dogs are said to have helped Noah by plugging leaking holes in his ark with their long noses.

- Fashion houses love to use Afghan Hounds in photo shoots with models because of their elegant appearance. Like human models, the dogs have their own portfolios of photographs and agents who handle their bookings.

German Shepherd Dog

- The German Shepherd Dog is one of the most popular dog breeds in the world. Its other names have been the Alsatian Wolf Dog and the Alsatian.

- Today's breed is descended from wolflike dogs in northern Germany that tended flocks of sheep. These dogs needed to have intelligence, endurance, and a quiet, calm nature to stop sheep from straying from their home pastures into neighboring fields of crops.

- German Shepherds make excellent guard dogs, and they can also be loyal and affectionate pets. They are active and athletic and need lots of exercise.

- One of the most famous German Shepherd Dogs is Rin Tin Tin. Found as a puppy on a French battlefield in the First World War, he was brought to the US by Lee Duncan, an American soldier. Duncan turned Rin Tin Tin into a Hollywood legend. The dog appeared in twenty-seven movies and has a star on the Hollywood Walk of Fame.

Fact file

Originates: Germany

Group: Herding

Height:
Females 22–24 in (56–61 cm)
Males 24–26 in (61–66 cm)

Weight:
Females 50–70 lb (23–32 kg)
Males 65–90 lb (30–41 kg)

Color: Usually black and tan; other colors include sable, black, and bicolor (with black the dominant color)

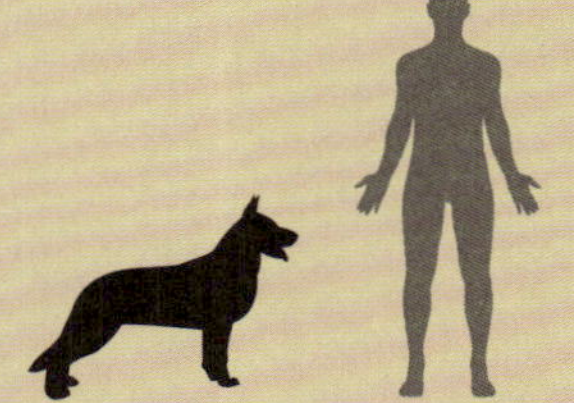

- In some countries, German Shepherds work as police dogs. They are used to catch suspects and protect officers working in dangerous situations.
- In 2021, a German Shepherd belonging to the UK charity the Guide Dogs for the Blind Association gave birth to twenty-four puppies, equaling the world record for litter size set in 2004.

Chihuahua

- For many years, the Chihuahua was considered the smallest dog in the world. Recently, the Russian Toy has become a recognized breed. It is a similar size but lighter in build.
- This breed is named after the Mexican state of Chihuahua. Although 70 percent of its genetic makeup is traceable to Mexican dogs, the other 30 percent is uncertain. Some experts suggest there are elements from Spain and China.
- Some small breeds, like the Chihuahua, are small and dainty enough to be carried around and to sit on your lap—although not all of them enjoy that!
- A Chihuahua's coat can either be short-haired or long-haired. Short-haired Chihuahuas have smooth, glossy fur. Some also have a neck ruff. Long-haired dogs have soft-textured fur that may be slightly wavy and a large neck ruff. They often have feathering, or a fringe of longer hair, in places like the ears, legs, and tail.
- The Chihuahua has a big personality, despite its size. Its happy and spirited nature and bright, alert eyes help to make it one of the most popular toy dogs.

Fact file

Originates: Mexico
Group: Toy
Height: 5–8 in (13–20 cm)
Weight: Up to 6 lb (3 kg)
Color: Any color

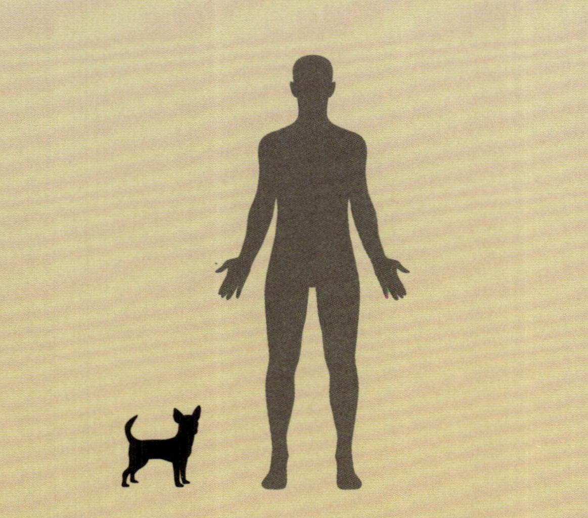

- All show dogs have domed heads with a well-defined stop—the place where the muzzle meets the forehead—and a short, slightly pointed muzzle. Pet dogs can have heads with a more gradual stop. These dogs also tend to be longer-legged and have larger ears.

Weimaraner

- Many gundogs are trained in just one skill—to seek out prey, to point out its location, or to retrieve it. The Weimaraner is a hunting dog that can do all three things.

- The striking silver-gray coat of the Weimaraner is unlike the coat of any other breed. It shimmers when the dog moves, giving the animal a ghostly appearance. This is emphasized by the Weimaraner's pale blue-gray or amber eyes.

- Weimaraners are often referred to as gray ghosts, partly because of their appearance, but also because they hunt silently. Unlike hounds, which bay continuously when following a scent, Weimaraners are stealthy and quiet while searching for prey, just like cats.

- Although Weimaraners are large, strong, and athletic, they are obedient and easy to train. They are excellent working dogs but, if kept as pets, they need plenty of space, exercise, and mental stimulation to be happy.

- The artist William Wegman is famous for taking photographs of his Weimaraners. He started to do this in the 1970s, dressing the dogs up as humans or characters from folk tales and nursery rhymes.

- Weimaraner puppies are born with light blue eyes and dark gray stripes. The tiger markings fade away in the first week after birth, but the eye color does not change until the puppies are about six months old.

Fact file

Originates: Germany

Group: Sporting

Height:
Females 23–25 in (58–64 cm)
Males 25–27 in (64–69 cm)

Weight:
Females 55–75 lb (25–35 kg)
Males 70–90 lb (32–41 kg)

Color: Gray

Dachshund

- This breed of dog is easily recognizable because of its long, narrow body and very short legs. Because of how they look, Dachshunds are sometimes referred to as weiners.

- Originally, all Dachshunds were smooth-coated dogs. The long-haired and wirehaired coats that we also see today were created later by cross-breeding with spaniels and terriers.

- Dachshunds can be either standard or miniature in size. They were once used for hunting because they could easily get into burrows. The larger standard dogs hunted badgers—*Dachshund* means "badger dog" in German. The smaller miniature dogs mainly caught rabbits.

- Slinky, the toy dog from Disney's Toy Story movies, is a Dachshund. The metal coil in the middle of his long body means he can stretch out to help his friends when they are in trouble.

Fact file

Originates: Germany

Group: Hound

Height:
Miniature 5–6 in (13–15 cm)
Standard 8–9 in (20–23 cm)

Weight:
Miniature up to 11 lb (5 kg)
Standard 16–32 lb (7–14.5 kg)

Color: Red, cream, wild boar; also black, chocolate, blue, and fawn (Isabella) with tan or cream markings

- Dachshunds are very intelligent and loyal. Despite their small size, they have big personalities. They make excellent guard dogs, as they are fearless and have a bark that sounds as if it comes from a much larger dog.

- In 2024 a new world record was set for the largest Dachshund dog walk. A dachshund-themed museum in Germany called Dackelmuseum arranged the dog walk through the city of Regensberg, in which 897 dogs and their owners paraded through the streets.

Tibetan Mastiff

- A mastifflike dog with strong protective instincts was developed as a watchdog hundreds of years ago in Tibet. Protected from below-freezing temperatures by its thick coat, it would be chained up outside so that it could alert people to any threats by barking.

- The modern Tibetan Mastiff is smaller than its ancestor, but it is still a powerfully built dog. It has an angular muzzle, a body that is slightly longer than it is tall, and a tail that is turned up over its back.

- The personality of today's Tibetan Mastiff is very different from the ancient breed. Over many generations, the dog has become much calmer and gentler. It is a loyal and loving companion.

- Tibetan Mastiffs are referred to as lion headed when they have very long hair that forms a mane on their forehead, neck, and shoulders. Dogs without this hair are called tiger headed.

Fact file

Originates: Chinese Tibet

Group: Working

Height:
Females 24–27 in (61–68.5 cm)
Males 26–29 in (66–73.5 cm)

Weight:
Females 70–120 lb (32–54 kg)
Males 90–150 lb (41–68 kg)

Color: Black, blue-gray, or brown (all with or without tan markings), gold

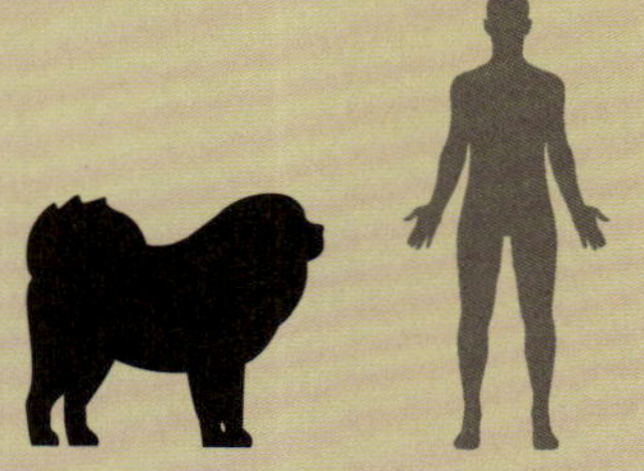

- As the Tibetan Mastiff is a heavily built dog with a long, dense coat, it is not suited to long walks, especially in hot weather. Two or three short outings a day are all that it needs.

- The most expensive dog ever sold is a Tibetan Mastiff. In 2011, a multimillionaire paid nearly $1,500,000 for an 11-month-old red puppy named Big Splash.

German Spitz

- Spitz dog breeds include the Japanese Shiba Inu and the Siberian Husky as well as the German Spitz. Most spitzes have thick coats, with a feathery tail that curls up and over their backs. Their upright, furry ears are usually quite small.

- In Germany, where this type of spitz originated, there are five varieties. From the largest to the smallest, these are the Wolfspitz, or Keeshond, the Großspitz (Giant), the Mittelspitz (Medium), the Kleinspitz (Miniature), and the Zwergspitz, or Pomeranian. Not all of these varieties are recognized in the same way in other countries.

- The German Spitz's coat has lots of long, woolly hair, which should stand away from the body. To achieve this effect, it should be groomed by brushing the coat against the direction of hair growth. Doing this also helps to prevent the fur from knotting and clumping together.

Fact file

Originates: Germany

Group: Miscellaneous

Height:
Miniature 8–12 in (20–30 cm)
Medium 12–16 in (30–40 cm)
Giant 16–20 in (40–51 cm)

Weight:
Miniature 10–11 lb (4.5–5 kg)
Medium 15–25 lb (7–11 kg)
Giant 30–50 lb (14–23 kg)

Color:
Miniature and Medium: black, brown, white, orange, orange sable, cream, gray-shaded, black and tan, particolors (two or more definite colors);
Giant: black, brown, white

- Cheerful, affectionate, lively, and eager to please, German Spitzes make ideal pets for people of all ages. Although energetic and playful, these dogs are easy to train and need only thirty to sixty minutes of exercise per day.

- German Spitzes shed their coat twice a year. This can be quite messy, as the dog will leave clumps of fur on almost everything it touches.

Rhodesian Ridgeback

- This South African breed originated from crosses between the native dogs of the indigenous Khoekhoe people and the dogs of the early Dutch and German settlers.
- Rhodesian Ridgebacks were once also called African lion dogs. They were bred to track large game, especially lions. The pack would either drive the big cats toward the hunters or corner and hold them until the hunters arrived.
- Rhodesian Ridgebacks get their name from the ridge of hair along their spine. It runs in the opposite direction from the rest of their sleek, glossy coat.
- Despite once being a courageous lion hunter, today's Ridgeback is a patient, reliable, and affectionate companion.

Fact file

Originates: South Africa

Group: Hound

Height:
Females 24–26 in (61–66 cm)
Males 25–27 in (63–69 cm)

Weight:
Females 70 lb (32 kg)
Males 85 lb (38.5 kg)

Color: Light to red wheaten

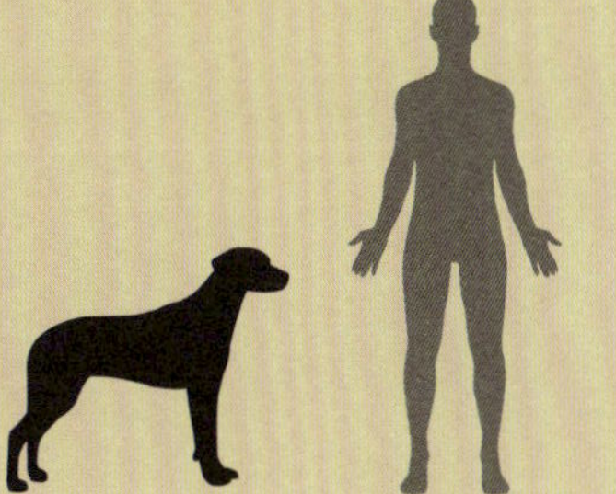

A large dog like this needs to be well trained from an early age. Puppies need to get used to being around people so that they grow to become good family dogs.

Old English Sheepdog

- The Old English Sheepdog has a surprising name because, like many breeds, it is not that old—it dates from about 1800. It is also more likely to work with cattle than with sheep.
- Underneath the dog's thick, shaggy coat is a compact, muscular, and athletic body. The eyes—when they can be seen—are dark brown or blue, or sometimes one of each.
- Since 1961, the Old English Sheepdog has been the mascot for Dulux, a British brand of paint. Starring in television and newspaper advertisements, the breed soon became known as the Dulux dog.
- The popularity of this gentle breed declined from the 1970s. So few puppies were being born that in 2020, it was put on a list of vulnerable breeds. Thankfully, numbers have now increased, and the Old English Sheepdog is no longer at risk.

Fact file

Originates: England

Group: Herding

Height:
Females at least 21 in (53 cm)
Males at least 22 in (56 cm)

Weight:
Females and males 60–100 lb (27–46 kg)

Color: Body and hindquarters any shade of gray, grizzle, blue, or blue merle, with a white head, neck, forelegs, and belly

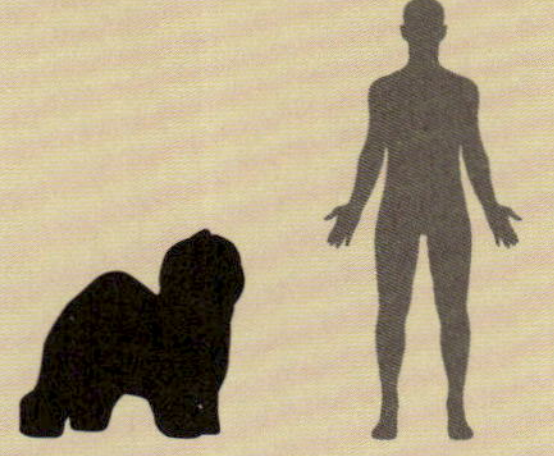

- When seen from behind, the Old English Sheepdog has a rolling, bearlike walk. Show dogs have their fur brushed up around their hindquarters to draw attention to this.
- Old English Sheepdogs have a loud and distinctive bark. It sounds like two pots being banged together.

Airedale Terrier

- The Airedale is the largest of the terriers. It takes its name from the Aire Valley in Yorkshire, UK, where it first came from.
- The Airedale Terrier has a long, flat head and powerful jaws. Its wiry coat lies close to the body and looks crinkly or slightly waved.
- This terrier was bred during the nineteenth century specifically to hunt rats and otters, which were considered a pest by local fishermen. A large, strong dog with endless stamina, it could easily keep up with the Otterhound pack it ran with.
- Airedales love swimming, even in cold water. This came in handy when a dog was trying to find the underwater entrance to an otter's burrow.
- During the First World War, thousands of Airedale Terriers were used by the Red Cross to find injured soldiers on the battlefield and carry medical supplies. They were also trained by the British Army to take messages along the trenches and transport carrier pigeons in crates strapped to their backs.

Fact file

Originates: England

Group: Terrier

Height: 23 in (59 cm)

Weight: 50–70 lb (23–32 kg)

Color: Tan with black or grizzle neck, saddle, and upper side of tail

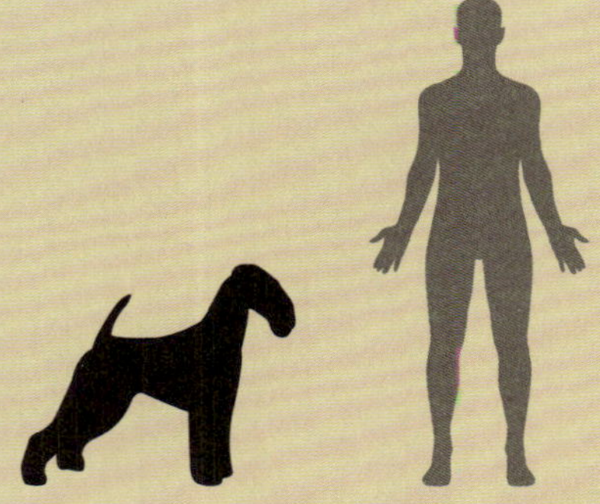

Although kind and gentle, Airedales can also be strong-minded and stubborn. They are generally keen to please, though, and, if trained correctly, are loyal family dogs.

Labrador Retriever

- The Labrador Retriever is a much-loved dog breed in North America and Europe and is also the most popular breed in the UK.
- The breed originated from dogs that helped fishermen in Newfoundland, Canada, bring in their nets. Some did this from the shore, while others worked from boats and swam to the beach towing the nets.
- Because of their calm temperaments, Labradors make excellent assistance dogs. They are trained to be guide dogs for the blind and hearing dogs for the deaf. They can be support dogs for people with physical disabilities and children with autism. Labradors also act as seizure-alert dogs for people with epilepsy.
- Labradors have a great sense of smell. This makes them ideal for detecting certain medical conditions and diseases, and for working with the armed forces to sniff out weapons, ammunition, and explosives.

Fact file

Originates: Canada

Group: Sporting

Height:
Females 21½–23½ in (54.5–60 cm)
Males 22½–24½ in (57–62 cm)

Weight:
Females 55–70 lb (25–32 kg)
Males 65–80 lb (30–36 kg)

Color: Yellow, black, chocolate

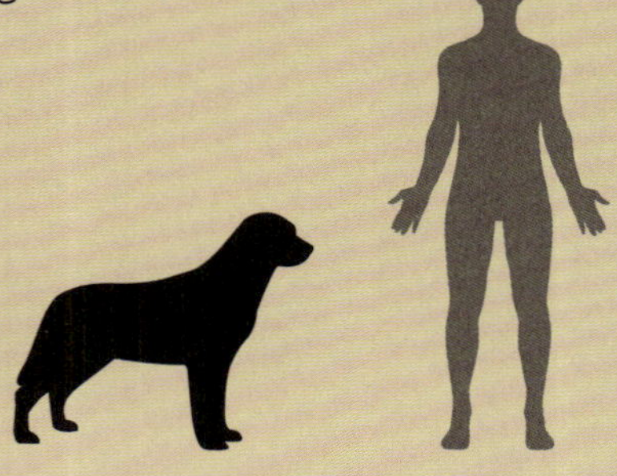

- Labradors generally have five to ten puppies in a litter, but very occasionally fourteen to seventeen puppies are born. At birth, each puppy weighs about 18 oz (500 g).

Pembroke Welsh Corgi

- There are two breeds of Welsh Corgi—the Pembroke and the Cardigan. The Pembroke Welsh Corgi has a slightly shorter body than the Cardigan Welsh Corgi and is more lightly built.

- Another way you might identify a Pembroke Corgi is by its colors. Most are red, but they can also be sable, fawn, or black and tan. Cardigan Corgis are mostly likely to be brindle or blue merle.

- Corgis used to be cattle-droving dogs in the Welsh hills and valleys. They worked the cattle from behind by nipping at their heels to make them move. Their agility and small size helped them dodge any kicks that the cattle tried to give them!

- The most famous owner of Pembroke Corgis was Elizabeth II, the late queen of the UK. She was given her first dog when she was seven. Over her long life, Queen Elizabeth owned and bred more than thirty Corgis.

Fact file

Originates: Wales

Group: Herding

Height: Females and males about 10–12 in (25–30 cm)

Weight:
Females up to 28 lb (12.5 kg)
Males up to 30 lb (14 kg)

Color: Red, sable, fawn, or black and tan, often with white head markings

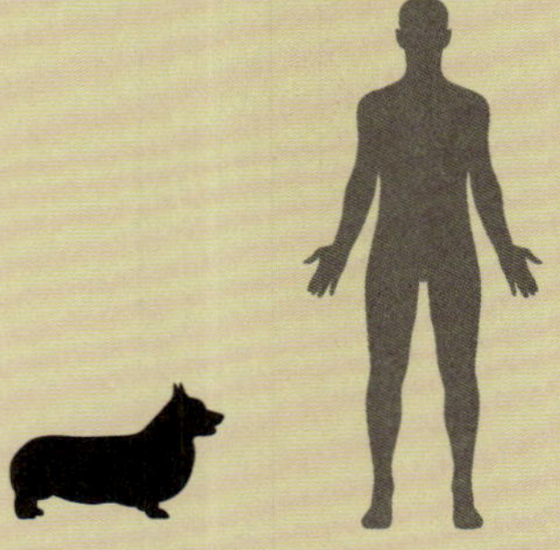

- Pembroke Corgis are friendly, outgoing dogs. They are also very energetic and love to play and explore new places. Despite their short legs, they enjoy going for long walks.

- At birth, a Pembroke Corgi's triangular ears are floppy. Over the next six months, the ears gradually stand up as the cartilage that supports them strengthens.

Siberian Husky

- There are more than twenty breeds of dog that are referred to as huskies, including the Alaskan Malamute and the Canadian Eskimo Dog. The Siberian Husky is the only one that is formally recognized as a husky by its name.

- Huskies come from the cold Arctic regions of the northern hemisphere, where winters are harsh and temperatures fall well below zero. They were bred to work in teams, pulling sleds through snow over long distances.

- Although some of their work is now done by snowmobiles, sled dogs are still essential in very remote areas in Russia, Canada, and Alaska, and in most of Greenland.

- The Siberian Husky was created in northeast Siberia by the Chukchi people. By using only their best sled dogs, they bred a lightly built husky that could cover large distances at high speed.

- As Siberian Huskies often live as well as work outside, they have very thick, well-insulated coats to keep them warm. Their ears, feet, and tail are also quite furry.

Siberian Huskies can be very vocal, although they rarely bark. Instead, they howl, yelp, whine, groan, and whimper. Each sound has a specific meaning, such as whining for attention when hurt.

Fact file

Originates: Russia

Group: Working

Height:
Females 20–22 in (51–56 cm)
Males 21–23½ in (53–60 cm)

Weight:
Females 35–50 lb (16–23 kg)
Males 45–60 lb (20–27 kg)

Color: All colors and markings except brindle and merle

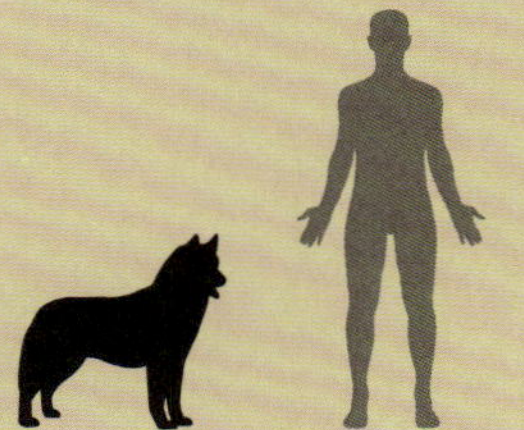

Greyhound

- The Greyhound is a gentle, sweet-natured sighthound that has been bred for speed. It has a slender, streamlined body, a relatively flat, narrow head, a deep chest, and long, powerful legs.

- Greyhounds were first used to hunt both large and small prey, including deer and hares. By the 1920s, they had become sporting dogs, racing each other around an oval track and sometimes jumping small fences, too.

- The Greyhound is the fastest of all dog breeds over a short distance and is thought to be the world's eighteenth-fastest land mammal. It can run as fast as 43 mph (70 km/h) and has great stamina and endurance.

- Dogs like the Greyhound have existed in many places for hundreds, if not thousands, of years. Slim, long-legged dogs similar to today's breed can be seen in the wall paintings of ancient Egyptian tombs.
- In 1931, the bus company Motor Transit Corporation changed its name to the Greyhound Corporation and chose the dog as its logo. No doubt it wanted its customers to think it had the fastest, most reliable buses.
- Despite their size and athletic ability, Greyhounds do not need a lot of exercise—just a walk twice a day.

Fact file

Originates: England

Group: Hound

Height:
Females 27–28 in (69–71 cm)
Males 28–30 in (71–76 cm)

Weight:
Females 60–65 lb (27–30 kg)
Males 65–70 lb (30–32 kg)

Color: Any color

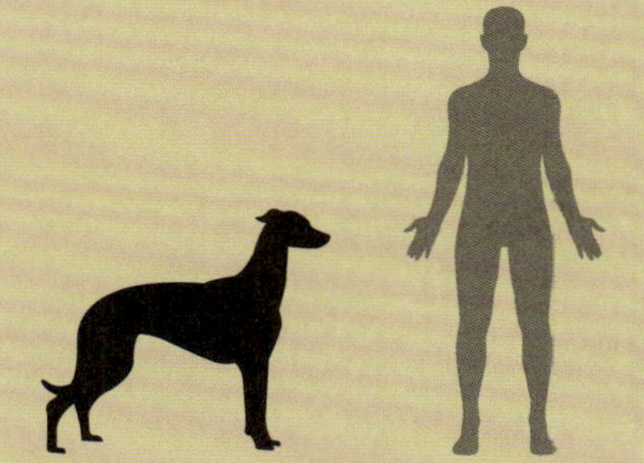

Australian Terrier

- This short-legged, coarse-coated terrier was created in the nineteenth century by early settlers in Australia. It was needed to help control the rats and mice that had been on board the ships the settlers had arrived on.

- The settlers crossed the various types of British terrier they had brought with them to create a tough new breed. The Australian Terrier had to be brave, intelligent, and hardworking in order to catch rodents both aboveground and belowground.

- Characteristic features of the Australian Terrier include a ruff of longer hair around its neck that extends down its chest, as well as a high-set tail. The coat is silky in some places and rough and wiry in others.

- Although it is still a working farm terrier, the Australian Terrier's temperament and character also make it a great companion.

- The Australian Terrier was one of the main breeds used to create a smaller pet dog—the Australian Silky Terrier. The new dog has kept the Australian Terrier's lively, fun-loving personality.

- The modern Australian Terrier still has the qualities that made it good at hunting rats. It is natural for it to dig if it picks up the scent of a burrowing animal. Keeping a dog well exercised and happy in the home will help stop it digging up the yard or park.

Fact file

Originates: Australia

Group: Terrier

Height: 10–11 in (25.5–28 cm)

Weight: 15–20 lb (7–9 kg)

Color: Shades of blue (including silver) with tan markings; sandy, red

Border Collie

- Many years ago, dogs known as collies herded sheep in the border country between Scotland and England. Today's Border Collies still herd all around the world.

- Border Collies are very intelligent and quickly learn how to herd sheep. They work silently, obeying the shouted or whistled commands of the shepherd. The main herding commands are to lie down, walk on, circle to the left or right, and stop and return.

- The Border Collie's coat can be either rough or smooth. The rough coat varies in length and is usually softer than the smooth coat. There is longer hair, known as feathering, on the front legs, chest, haunches, and underside.

- As pets, Border Collies need plenty of exercise and mental stimulation to keep them happy. With good training, they can become loyal and obedient companions that enjoy the company of people and dogs.

Chaser was a Border Collie that knew the names of more than a thousand objects. She demonstrated this by fetching one of the objects when asked. Chaser is considered to have the biggest memory of any animal apart from humans.

As well as being skillful at herding sheep, Border Collies are excellent search-and-rescue dogs. They are hard workers and very easy to train.

Fact file

Originates: Scotland

Group: Herding

Height:
Females 18–21 in (46–53 cm)
Males 19–22 in (48–56 cm)

Weight:
Females and males 30–55 lb (14–25 kg)

Color: Various

Chinese Crested

- There are only a few hairless dog breeds. Unlike the others, the Chinese Crested has some hair on its head, tail, and feet. The head hair is called a crest, the tail hair is a plume, and the foot hair is known as a sock.

- Most hairless breeds originated in Latin America, although some come from Africa and India. Studies of the Chinese Crested suggest that the dog's ancestors original y came from Mexico. China was trading with Mexico at least four hundred years ago, so it is possible that traders took these little dogs back home with them on their ships.

- Some Chinese Crested dogs have a full coat known as the powderpuff. The short, soft undercoat is protected by longer, straight guard hairs. Both hairless and furry puppies can be born in the same litter.

- A small, athletic dog with a delightful temperament, the Chinese Crested attracts attention wherever it goes. It is a gentle, affectionate dog that loves to play and is generally good with people and other animals.

- A hairless Chinese Crested does not need much grooming, but it should have frequent baths. They dry much more quickly than dogs with fur!

- Because they have no hair, Chinese Cresteds get cold in winter, and in summer, their bare skin is easily sunburned. A warm dog coat and dog-friendly sunscreen will help to protect them in each season.

- Small dogs can be yappy and tend to bark more than larger dogs. The Chinese Crested is less vocal than some of the other toy dog breeds.

Fact file

Originates: China

Group: Toy

Height: 11–13 in (28–33 cm)

Weight: 8–12 lb (3.5–5 kg)

Color: Any color or color combination

Dalmatian

With its spectacular spotted white coat, the Dalmatian is the most easily recognizable of all the dog breeds. The spots are either black or liver in color—liver is a rich brown shade. Mostly, the spots are about 1 inch (2.5 cm) across, but some dogs have larger patches of color on their ears.

When Dalmatian puppies are born, they have plain white fur. Although spots may be visible on their skin, they do not appear on their coats until the puppies are one to two weeks old.

Nobody is sure where this breed originally came from. Spotted dogs are known to have existed in ancient India and Egypt as well as in several European countries. Recent studies suggest the Dalmatian is most closely related to the Istrian Hound from Croatia and the English Greyhound.

Slim and muscular, Dalmatians have great endurance. Many years ago in England, they were used as carriage dogs. They tirelessly kept pace alongside horse-drawn vehicles to protect wealthy passengers from robbers. Their elegant appearance soon made owning a Dalmatian the height of fashion—and a display of their owner's high status.

Fact file

Originates: Unknown

Group: Non-Sporting

Height: 19–23 in (48–58 cm)

Weight: 45–70 lb (20–32 kg)

Color: White with round black or liver spots

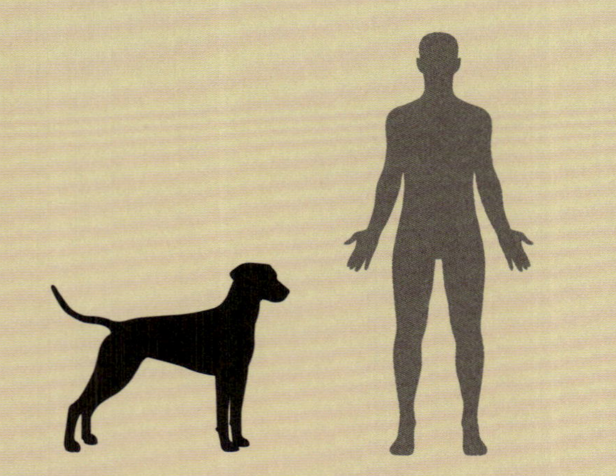

Dalmatians tend to have larger litters of puppies than many breeds, usually ranging from eight to ten. In 2019, the largest Dalmation litter ever was born in Australia. There were nineteen puppies—nine females and ten males.

The book *The Hundred and One Dalmatians* by Dodie Smith was published in 1956, telling the tale of the kidnap of fifteen adorable Dalmatian puppies. It was made into a cartoon movie by Walt Disney in 1961 and a live-action movie in 1996.

Scottish Terrier

- The lively Scottish Terrier is known for its characterful bushy eyebrows and long beard. It is affectionately known as a Scottie.
- Scottish Terriers were bred in Perthshire, Scotland, to hunt rats and other pests. As working farm dogs, they were fearless and efficient.
- This breed has a rough coat and compact, muscular body. Despite having short legs, Scotties are active dogs that enjoy brisk walks and games.
- A black Scottish Terrier named Jock is one of the characters in the Disney movie *Lady and the Tramp*. He lives in the house next door to Lady and becomes one of her friends.
- At the 2014 Commonwealth Games opening ceremony in Glasgow, Scottish Terriers led out the teams. Each dog wore a tartan coat bearing the name of a participating country. Since there were seventy-one nations taking part but only forty-one dogs, some of the Scotties had to have a very quick costume change!

- Famous owners of Scotties have included the UK's Queen Victoria, the writer and illustrator Beatrix Potter, and several US presidents.
- The Scottie is one of the most popular playing pieces in the board game Monopoly. Over the years, other pieces have been replaced—but not this iconic little dog.

Fact file

Originates: Scotland

Group: Terrier

Height: Females and males about 10 in (25 cm)

Weight:
Females 18–21 lb (8–9.5 kg)
Males 19–22 lb (8.5–10 kg)

Color: Black, brindle, wheaten

Irish Setter

- With its stunning, glossy red coat, the Irish Setter is probably the most glamorous of all dog breeds. It is also the most popular type of setter.
- Irish Setters are outgoing, friendly, and eager to please. This makes them easy to train.
- These large dogs have lots of energy and need plenty of exercise.
- Ancestors of the Irish Setter were used to hunt gamebirds, such as quail and pheasant. The dogs were trained to track down a bird by scent, then to crouch down facing the bird until a net was set to catch it.
- Irish Setters love to play. Hunting is a natural behavior for gundogs like these, so running after and retrieving balls is one of their favorite games.

Irish Setters are happy to go out in all kinds of weather. Their silky coats can easily become tangled while the dogs are exploring their surroundings. They need regular brushing to keep them in good condition.

Fact file

Originates: Ireland

Group: Sporting

Height:
Females 25 in (63.5 cm)
Males 27 in (68.5 cm)

Weight:
Females 60 lb (27 kg)
Males 70 lb (32 kg)

Color: Mahogany, rich chestnut

Bichon Frise

- Today's Bichon Frise is descended from little white dogs that were brought to the island of Tenerife from the Spanish mainland in the early fifteenth century. They were often kept as lapdogs by noblewomen.
- Three other small, white companion dog breeds are associated with islands—the Maltese of Malta, the Coton de Tulear of Madagascar, and the Havanese of Cuba.
- The Bichon Frise is a sturdy dog with a rounded head and long, fluffy ears that drop down on each side. Standing out against its soft white coat are dark eyes, a black nose, and black-rimmed eyes and lips. The plumed tail is carried up over its back.
- The Bichon Frise's soft, dense undercoat and long, curly topcoat need daily brushing to deal with tangles and prevent matting. It is important to get a puppy used to being groomed before its adult coat develops.
- Bichon Frises are cheerful and playful dogs. Although they bark a lot and can be quite feisty, they tend not to make very good guard dogs, as they are friendly and inquisitive.

Fact file

Originates: Spain
Group: Non-Sporting
Height: 9½–11½ in (24–29 cm)
Weight: 12–18 lb (5–8 kg)
Color: White

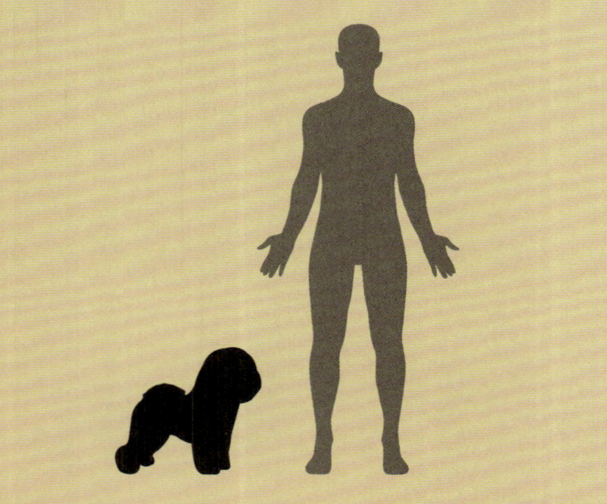

- These are sociable dogs that prefer to be around people. Bichons are intelligent and like to please their owners, so they are quick and willing to learn.
- The English name for this breed comes from the French description *bichon à poil frisé*, meaning "curly-haired small dog."

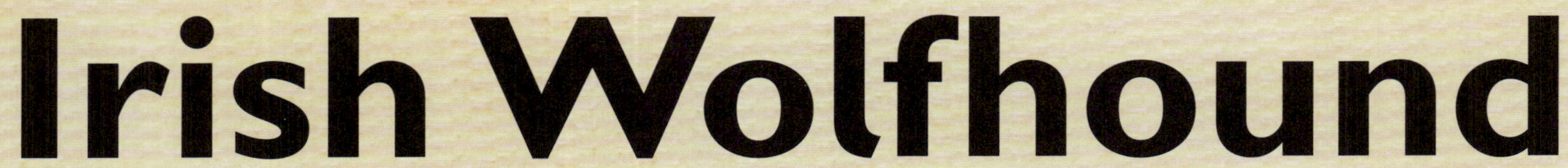

Irish Wolfhound

- In the past, huge, rough-coated dogs were used in Ireland to hunt wolves. When there were no wolves left to hunt, the dogs were no longer needed. By the mid-nineteenth century, hardly any of these early wolfhounds still existed.

- The modern Irish Wolfhound was developed from the Deerhound, which has a similar coat and color, and the Great Dane, which probably gave the wolfhound its large size. The Greyhound, Borzoi, and Tibetan Mastiff were also used.

- Irish Wolfhounds are one of the tallest breeds of dog. The tallest known dog, named Murphy, measured over 38 inches (96 cm) at the shoulder—more than half the height of a grown man!

- The mascot of the British Army's Irish Guards is an Irish Wolfhound. In 2020, Turlough Mór, named after an ancient Irish king, became the seventeenth dog to take on this role.

- Irish Wolfhounds are gentle giants that rarely bark. They are often used as guard dogs, but it is their size rather than the noise they make that is most likely to frighten burglars!

Very big dogs like these need plenty of space to move around. Irish Wolfhounds can be a bit lazy, so daily outings will keep them in good shape.

Fact file

Originates: Ireland

Group: Hound

Height:
Females at least 30 in (76 cm)
Males at least 32 in (81 cm)

Weight:
Females at least 105 lb (47.5 kg)
Males at least 120 lb (54.5 kg)

Color: Gray, brindle, red, black, fawn, wheaten, steel gray, pure white

Russell Terrier

- This breed is the smaller of two closely related terriers named after a parson, or clergyman, named John (Jack) Russell. A keen hunter, Russell wanted to create a working terrier that could run with a pack of hounds and flush foxes from their dens.

- For nearly two hundred years, all small white terriers with black or tan markings were referred to as Jack Russell Terriers. Nowadays, the dogs with squarer bodies and longer legs are called Parson Russell Terriers, with the smaller dogs known just as Russell Terriers.

- Russell Terriers are highly intelligent. Many learn to tip their head to one side when their owners speak to them. They seem to know that this makes them more endearing, which could result in more food or playtime.

- There are three different coat types for this breed—smooth, broken, and rough. Rough-coated dogs have a fuller beard and eyebrows and thicker leg hair.

- Russell Terriers are cheerful, energetic dogs that enjoy going for walks. They love to play, especially if it involves using their hunting instinct to find hidden treats.

Fact file

Originates: England

Group: Terrier

Height: 10–12 in (25–30 cm)

Weight: 9–15 lb (4–7 kg)

Color: Mainly white with black and/or tan markings

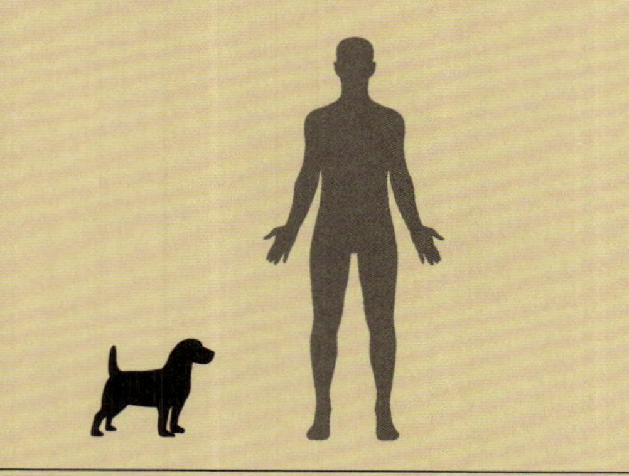

- Because they were initially bred as working dogs, Russell Terriers are happiest when they are doing something. If they are bored, they may bark more than they should.

Newfoundland

- The Newfoundland dog takes its name from the area in northeastern Canada where it was first bred. These dogs pulled carts of fish from the docks to the market and brought logs from the forest for settlers to use as fuel. They also worked in the water, retrieving fishing nets and lost equipment.

- Today's Newfoundland is a large, extremely affectionate dog. It needs plenty of indoor and outdoor space to live in.

- In J. M. Barrie's book *Peter Pan*, the dog Nana, who looks after the three children of the Darling family, is a Newfoundland. When Disney made a film version of the book, the dog was changed to a St. Bernard.

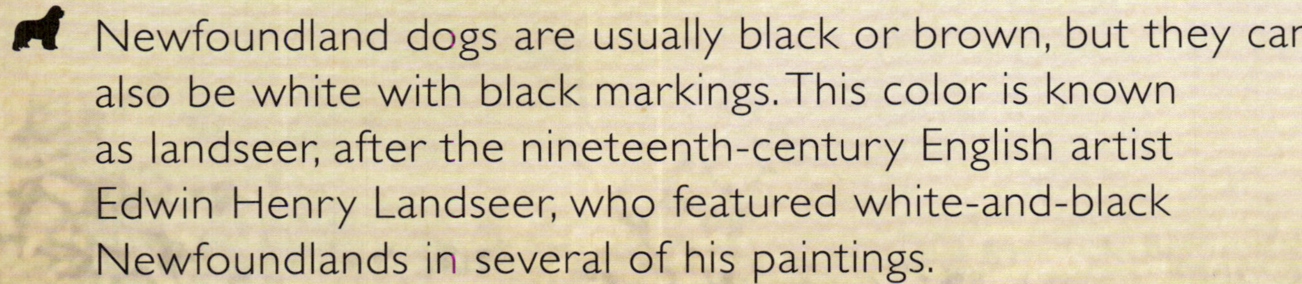

- Newfoundland dogs are usually black or brown, but they can also be white with black markings. This color is known as landseer, after the nineteenth-century English artist Edwin Henry Landseer, who featured white-and-black Newfoundlands in several of his paintings.

Fact file

Originates: Canada

Group: Working

Height:
Females about 26 in (66 cm)
Males about 28 in (71 cm)

Weight:
Females 100–120 lb (46–54 kg)
Males 130–150 lb (59–68 kg)

Color: Black, brown, gray, landseer

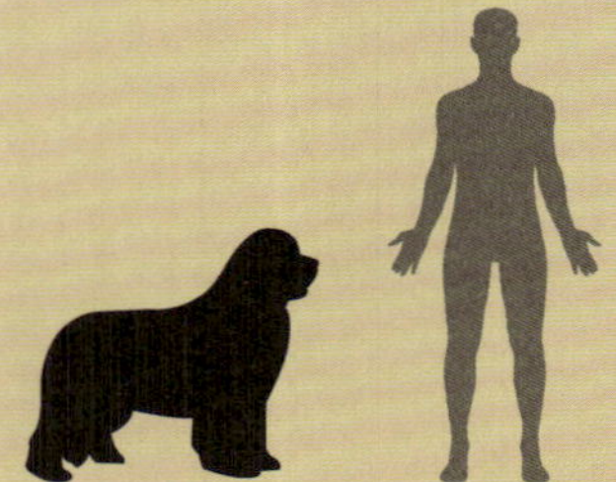

Newfoundlands are excellent swimmers. They have an oily, waterproof coat and partially webbed feet to help them power through the water. Calm and strong, they have even jumped out of helicopters to rescue people from drowning.

Bull Terrier

- Bull Terriers have a distinctive egg-shaped head that slopes from the top of the skull to the tip of the nose. It looks like this because there is no stop—an indentation where the muzzle meets the forehead.

- The ancestors of this breed were fighting dogs created in the nineteenth century by crossing Old English Bulldogs with terriers. The new dogs were fast, fearless, intelligent, and tenacious.

- Over time, other breeds were crossed with the early fighting dogs to create a dog with a calmer nature. These dogs had smooth white coats—like some of today's Bull Terriers. They were known as white cavaliers and were very successful in dog shows.

- Although the white dogs were popular, in the early twentieth century, people started to breed Bull Terriers with brindle coloring. This is where the top coat has a pattern of black stripes over a lighter-colored base coat.

- Bull Terriers are known for their courage, power, and agility. They have stocky bodies and walk in a jaunty way. Playful and mischievous, they can also be quite stubborn but are always devoted to their owners.

- Bull Terriers with white coloring are more likely than others to be deaf because they have something called a piebald gene. Breeds such as Boxers and Dalmatians have this, too—but not all white dogs are deaf.

- There used to be three sizes of Bull Terrier—standard, miniature, and toy. The toy became extinct in the early twentieth century, so now only two types remain.

Fact file

Originates: England

Group: Terrier

Height:
Miniature 10–14 in (25–35.5 cm)
Standard 21–22 in (53–56 cm)

Weight: 50–70 lb (23–32 kg)

Color: White and black, red, fawn, tricolor, brindle

Chow Chow

- The Chow Chow is probably the oldest East Asian dog breed. It is one of the few dogs to have a blue-black tongue and lips.
- Chow Chow puppies are born with pink tongues. The tongues only get their characteristic dark color as the puppies get older.
- In ancient China, Chow Chows were used for hunting, guarding property, and pulling carts.
- Chow Chows have dense fur that can be either long or short. In the long-haired dogs, the fur forms a ruff around the neck that looks a bit like a lion's mane.
- The Chow Chow has a calm, quiet nature. It seems very dignified, partly due to the stiff-legged way it walks. The hind legs stay straight and swing from the hip like the pendulum of a grandfather clock.

Fact file

Originates: China
Group: Non-Sporting
Height: 17–20 in (43–51 cm)
Weight: 45–70 lb (20–32 kg)
Color: Black, blue, red, cinnamon, cream

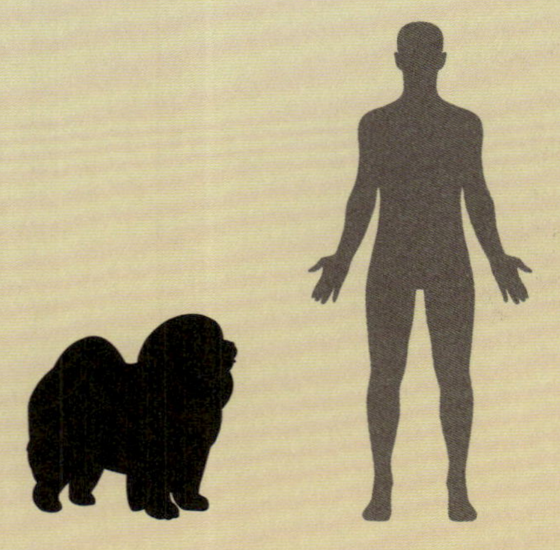

- The average litter size for Chow Chows is four to six puppies, but occasionally there are more. In 2018, a Chow Chow named Bushka had a litter of eleven puppies, which was thought to be a record for the breed.
- Even though they look as cuddly as teddy bears, Chow Chows are not very affectionate. They can be quite stubborn and aloof, which can make training a challenge.

Great Dane

- Great Danes are very large. They are descended from German dogs, not Danish ones, despite their name. Those dogs were once used to hunt wild boar.
- The Great Dane has two distinct characteristics. One is long legs and the other is a rectangular head that is held high on a long, almost upright neck.
- The Great Dane's handsome, regal appearance has led to its nickname, the Apollo of dogs. In ancient Greek mythology, the sun god Apollo was considered the most beautiful of all the gods.
- These gentle giants are friendly, tolerant, and good with children. Because of their great size and strength, Great Danes need to be well trained from birth.
- Great Danes have a short, smooth coat. The harlequin color—white with black or blue patches—is less common than the other colors. Two harlequin-colored dogs will not necessarily have harlequin puppies.

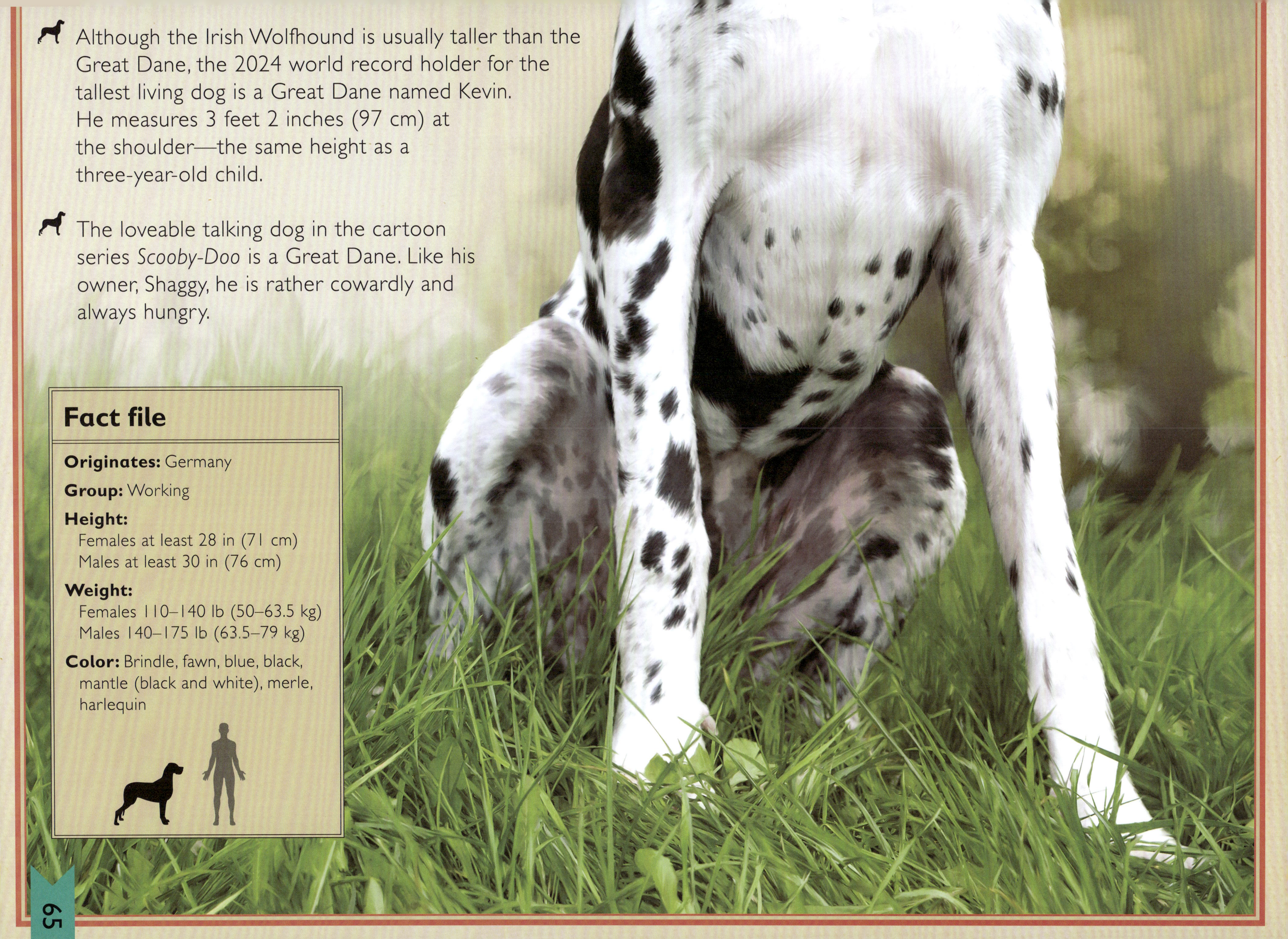

- Although the Irish Wolfhound is usually taller than the Great Dane, the 2024 world record holder for the tallest living dog is a Great Dane named Kevin. He measures 3 feet 2 inches (97 cm) at the shoulder—the same height as a three-year-old child.
- The loveable talking dog in the cartoon series *Scooby-Doo* is a Great Dane. Like his owner, Shaggy, he is rather cowardly and always hungry.

Fact file

Originates: Germany

Group: Working

Height:
Females at least 28 in (71 cm)
Males at least 30 in (76 cm)

Weight:
Females 110–140 lb (50–63.5 kg)
Males 140–175 lb (63.5–79 kg)

Color: Brindle, fawn, blue, black, mantle (black and white), merle, harlequin

Poodle

- The Poodle originated in Germany, where it was used to retrieve waterfowl, such as ducks. Its name comes from the German word *Pudeln*, which means "to splash."

- Most Poodles have dense, curly coats that can be any solid color. These dogs should be brushed every day to prevent the coat from becoming knotted or matted. A small number of poodles have corded coats, which are cared for in a different way.

- Poodles are a popular choice to cross with other breeds because of their low-shedding coats. There are now about forty cross-bred types, including the Labradoodle, which is a Poodle crossed with a Labrador Retriever, and the Cockapoo, which is a Poodle–Cocker Spaniel cross.

- Poodles also have a long association with France. It was here that the Poodle became the elegant breed of dog we know today.

Fact file

Originates: Germany

Group: Toy/Non-Sporting

Height:
Toy up to 10 in (25 cm)
Miniature 10–15 in (25–38 cm)
Standard at least 15 in (38 cm)

Weight:
Toy females and males
4–6 lb (2–3 kg)
Miniature females and males
10–15 lb (4.5–7 kg)
Standard females
40–50 lb (18–23 kg);
males 60–70 lb (27–32 kg)

Color: Solid colors, including black, blue, gray, silver, brown, red, apricot, cream, white

- There are four sizes of Poodle—standard, medium, miniature, and toy. The medium-sized variety is not recognized in many countries.

- A Poodle's coat can be clipped in various ways, such as giving the dog a pompon tail and fluffy "bracelets" to protect the ankles. Show dogs have more extravagant clips compared to those of pet dogs.

Cocker Spaniel

- The Cocker Spaniel was bred from the English Cocker Spaniels that were brought to what is now the US by the early English settlers. Those dogs were used to flush out and retrieve gamebirds, such as woodcocks and grouse.

- Cocker Spaniels are smaller and more lightly built and have longer, silkier coats than English Cocker Spaniels in the UK. The head is rounder, with prominent eyebrows, a well-defined stop, and a shorter, deeper muzzle.

- The Cocker Spaniel's spectacular coat needs a lot of attention to prevent it from matting. The feathering on the ears, chest, abdomen, and legs is best seen in show dogs, whose coats are longer and always very well groomed.

- As well as being good-looking, the Cocker Spaniel is sweet-natured, cheerful, and friendly. It loves to play but is not overly boisterous. These characteristics make it an ideal companion or family dog.

- The Cocker Spaniel is one of the most popular dog breeds. Famous owners have included the talk show host Oprah Winfrey and actor George Clooney.

- Cocker Spaniels are happy in the city or in the countryside. They still have the hunting instincts of their ancestors and so can be tempted to chase things when they are off the leash. It is important that they learn the recall skill early in their training.

Newborn puppies weigh ½ to 1 lb (0.25 to 0.5 kg). They will grow to more than three times this size within their first month.

Fact file

Originates: United States

Group: Sporting

Height:
Females 13½–14½ in (34–37 cm)
Males 14½–15½ in (37–39 cm)

Weight:
Females 20–25 lb (9–11 kg)
Males 25–30 lb (11–14 kg)

Color: Any solid color, black or brown and tan, particolors (two or more definite colors)

Rottweiler

- Like many dog breeds, the Rottweiler takes its name from the place it first came from—the town of Rottweil in southwest Germany. There is a bronze statue of a Rottweiler outside the town's museum to celebrate the breed.

- Rottweilers are powerfully built and have a sleek, black coat with red to mahogany markings. These include a spot above each eye and on each cheek, and a strip around each side of the muzzle. There are more markings on the chest, legs, and tail.

- Strong, intelligent, loyal, and courageous, Rottweilers need firm and experienced owners to train them properly from puppyhood. They can be good-natured and loving family dogs.

- Rottweilers were originally cattle-droving dogs, helping to take valuable livestock to market for sale. On the way back, drovers would sometimes attach their money bags to their dog's collar to protect their precious cash from robbers.
- Due to their imposing stature and protective nature, Rottweilers make excellent guard dogs. Their bark is loud and fierce but is usually only used as a warning when the dogs sense danger.
- Rottweilers are used by the police and military for jobs that involve guarding and defending.

Fact file

Originates: Germany

Group: Working

Height:
Females 22–25 in (56–64 cm)
Males 24–27 in (61–69 cm)

Weight:
Females 80–100 lb (36–46 kg)
Males 95–135 lb (43–61 kg)

Color: Black with defined tan markings

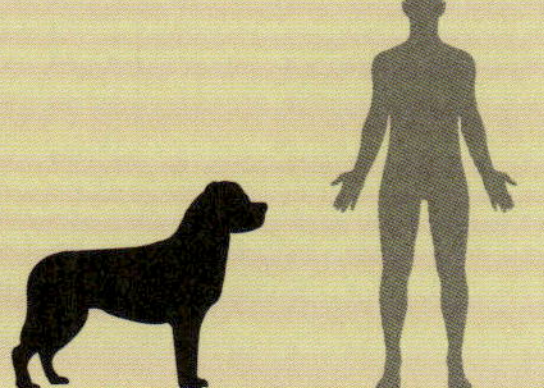

Shiba Inu

- Most dog breeds cannot be traced back further than the nineteenth century, but experts believe the Shiba Inu originated much earlier than that.

- The Shiba Inu was originally bred to hunt small game, especially ground-nesting birds. It occasionally helped in tackling larger animals, such as wild boar.

- Many Shiba Inus were killed in the Second World War or died from a disease called canine distemper. Breeding programs set up using the few surviving dogs saved the breed from extinction.

- The confident and good-natured Shiba Inu is one of the most popular companion dogs in Japan. It has been the country's national dog since 1937.

- Several Shiba Inus have social media accounts with a large number of followers. This has helped to spread the breed's popularity to other countries.

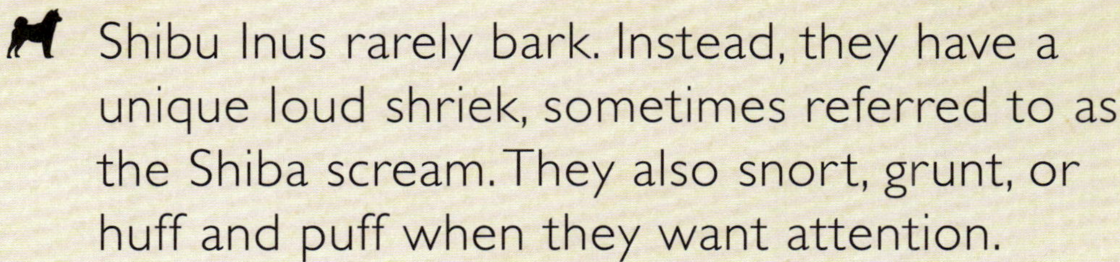

Shibu Inus rarely bark. Instead, they have a unique loud shriek, sometimes referred to as the Shiba scream. They also snort, grunt, or huff and puff when they want attention.

Despite their aloof appearance, Shiba Inus are inquisitive and love to play. Nimble and quick, they also like to go for long walks. They need to be on a leash if there is wildlife nearby, as they have a strong hunting instinct.

Fact file

Originates: Japan

Group: Non-Sporting

Height:
Females 13½–15½ in (34–39 cm)
Males 14½–16½ in (37–42 cm)

Weight:
Females about 17 lb (7.5 kg)
Males about 23 lb (10.5 kg)

Color: Red, black and tan, sesame

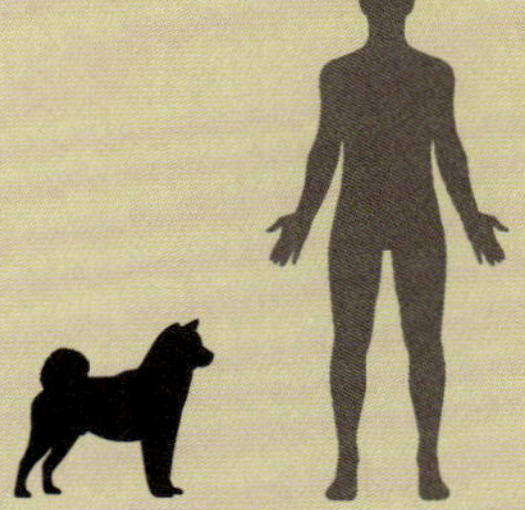

Puli

- The Puli is best known for its stunning, floor-length, corded coat. Black is the most common color, but dogs can also be gray, fawn, or white.
- The ancestors of the Puli are thought to have come from Siberia. These dogs were brought to Hungary by a nomadic people called the Magyars, who settled in the treeless, grassy plains known as the Puszta.
- There were no fences on the Puszta, so good herding dogs were essential for controlling a shepherd's flock. At night, a large white dog guarded the sheep. During the day a smaller, nimbler dog kept the flock together and moved it to fresh pastures when necessary. The smaller dogs eventually became today's Puli.
- Pulis are intelligent, high-energy dogs that need plenty of exercise to keep them happy. They should have interesting walks of one to two hours per day and a secure yard to run around in and explore.
- A Puli's corded coat needs a lot of care and is generally only seen in show dogs. Pet dogs are more likely to have dreadlocks rather than cords.

Fact file

Originates: Hungary

Group: Herding

Height:
Females 15–17 in (38–43 cm)
Males 16–18 in (40–46 cm)

Weight: Females and males 25–35 lb (11–16 kg)

Color: Rusty black, black, all shades of gray, white

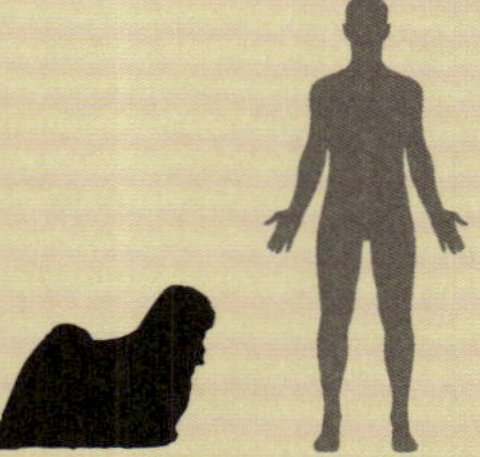

Their history as a herding dog makes Pulis very independent and wary of strangers, so they need to be trained well from an early age. They quickly learn to obey hand signals and voice commands.

Beagle

- Scenthounds use their sense of smell rather than their sight to locate and track game animals, such as rabbits. The Beagle is one of the smaller scenthound breeds and so is able to follow a scent trail through denser undergrowth than the larger hunting dogs can.

- Beagles, like most scenthounds, have large drop ears—they hang down at the sides of the head. Their coat is short, dense, and waterproof. Beagles have the typical tricolor hound colorings of black, tan, and white markings.

- Its attractive appearance, compact build, and cheerful nature make the Beagle a popular choice as a pet.

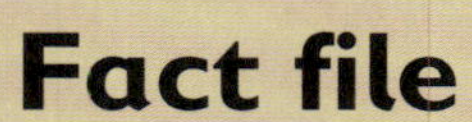

Fact file

Originates: England

Group: Hound

Height: Up to 15 in (38 cm)

Weight: Up to 30 lb (14 kg)

Color: Tricolor, including black or blue, with tan and white; bicolor, including lemon, red, or black, with white; all white

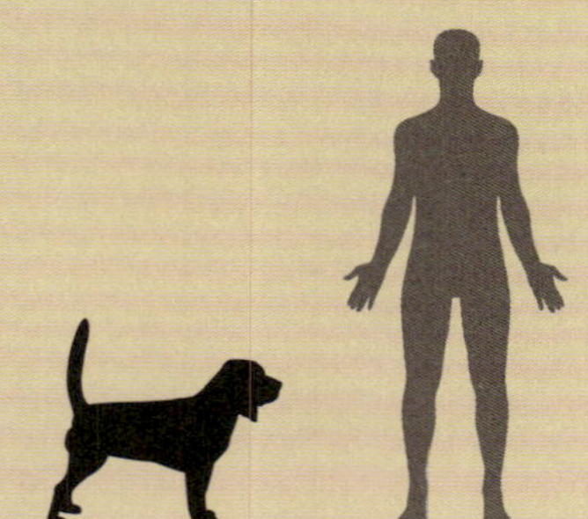

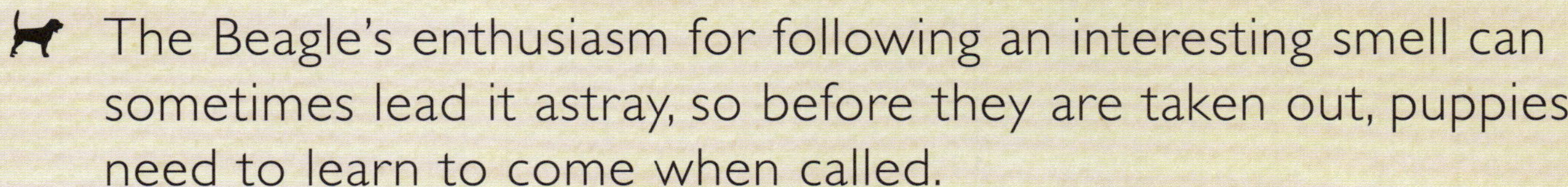

- The Beagle's enthusiasm for following an interesting smell can sometimes lead it astray, so before they are taken out, puppies need to learn to come when called.
- The famous character of Snoopy, from the cartoon strip *Peanuts,* is a Beagle. Snoopy was based on the artist Charles M. Schulz's own dog, Spike.

Boxer

- The Boxer is a medium-sized, powerfully built dog. Its strong muscles can easily be seen under its short, smooth coat.
- A Boxer's most distinctive feature is its short muzzle. There are wrinkles at its base that run down each side of its face.
- Boxers were used during the First and Second World Wars as messengers and pack carriers. They became popular as pets in the 1940s, when some of the returning soldiers took the dogs home with them.
- Easy to train and even-tempered, Boxers make excellent pets. They are also good guard dogs, as they are fearless and protective of their family and home.
- At full speed, Boxers can run at 30 mph (50 km/h). They may not be as speedy as Greyhounds, but they are faster than a world-champion 100-meter sprinter!
- In 2023, a male Boxer named Rocky was recognized as having the longest tongue of any living dog. It measured 5.47 inches (13.89 cm), beating the previous record by nearly ½ inch (1.3 cm).

Boxers are intelligent and curious and have lots of energy. They need plenty of outside space to run around in and explore.

Fact file

Originates: Germany

Group: Working

Height:
Females 21½–23½ in (54.5–60 cm)
Males 23–25 in (58–63 cm)

Weight:
Females about 55–60 lb (25–27 kg)
Males about 66–70 lb (30–32 kg)

Color: Fawn, brindle

Dog Breed Groups

Dog breeds were originally developed to carry out specific tasks. These tasks are used to allocate them to a particular group.

Hound
Hounds are breeds that were originally used for hunting. Dogs hunt either by scent or by sight. Hounds are often described as dignified and aloof.

Dachshund

Afghan Hound

Greyhound

Beagle

Irish Wolfhound

Rhodesian Ridgeback

Terrier
Terriers were originally used to hunt vermin, such as rats, foxes, badgers, and otters. They are very brave and tough.

Airedale Terrier

Russell Terrier

Scottish Terrier

Australian Terrier

Bull Terrier

Sporting
These breeds were originally trained to find live game or bring back game that had been shot. They include Spaniels, Retrievers, Pointers, and Setters.

Irish Setter

Cocker Spaniel

Golden Retriever

Labrador Retriever

Weimaraner

Working
Working breeds were originally used to protect and guard people and property, or to pull carts or sleds. They are large, muscular, and very strong.

Boxer

Great Dane

Tibetan Mastiff

Siberian Husky

Newfoundland

Rottweiler

Herding
This group consists of breeds that herd animals such as cattle, sheep, and reindeer. The dogs usually have a double coat to help keep their bodies warm and dry when working outside.

Old English Sheepdog

Border Collie

Puli

Pembroke Welsh Corgi

German Shepherd Dog

Non-Sporting
This group of breeds is very varied. It includes dogs that were bred for a purpose not included in the other groups. Some of the breeds are the oldest in the world.

French Bulldog

Shiba Inu

Chow Chow

Bichon Frise

Poodle

Dalmatian

Toy
Toy breeds are small companion dogs, sometimes known as lapdogs. They are usually very friendly and love attention, and generally need shorter daily walks than larger breeds.

Chihuahua

Chinese Crested

Miscellaneous
Breeds in this group are working toward formal acceptance by the American Kennel Club. Once it has met a number of criteria, it will become a recognized breed.

German Spitz